Passive Income

Legitimate Income Opportunities
Build Lifetime of Passive
Income in less than
6 Months

Lance MacNeil

Table of Contents

Introduction

People with jobs believe that their 'income' is representative of their wealth. The questions they ask are "who do you work for?" "How much do you earn?" or "what car do you drive?"

These people fall into the category of "looking good, going nowhere". They buy stuff to look and feel rich. To sustain their lifestyle they continually work harder, longer hours and constantly educate themselves to become even more specialized.

A paycheck, no matter how big, cannot be defined as wealth or riches. Most people think that getting a bigger paycheck or salary is making them richer. Nothing can be further from truth. In fact 95% of people spend every dollar they earn. By the way acronym for job is "Just Over Broke"

We need 'cash flow' to pay our bills, put food on the table, send our kids to school and sustain any kind of lifestyle. But if your 'cash flow' is solely reliant on your paycheck then you are at grave risk. You can fall ill, have an accident or lose your job. Ask millions who have lost their jobs in the financial downturn.

Having a job severely restricts your cash flow capabilities. You can work for only 'X' hours in a day. Your pay check will be limited to number of hours worked multiplied by your hourly rate.

Your first step to creating wealth comes when your 'cash flow' starts coming from passive income rather than paycheck. In other words, your investments and businesses pay you money whether you set out of bed or not.

Your next step forward is to create long term passive income cash flow backed by solid asset base. Wealth is all about owning assets. However an asset must have both capital growth and income. Don't buy property first if you want to become rich or you will become 'asset rich' and 'cash poor'. You must first concentrate on generating a rather large passive income. Cash flow not only supports your lifestyle but also has the ability to get loans to buy income producing assets.

Passive cash flow is generated out of investments (paper assets or properties that are fully paid for), businesses that have systems in place and do not require your day to day presence, or your income generated as a result of royalties from intellectual property rights that you have created. To grow rich you have to make either money or people work for you even when you sleep or are holidaying on the beach.

The quickest way to become rich fast is to generate massive cash flow through a business that has proven systems. You then have to buy assets that give you not only passive income but also capital appreciation. If you do not have a huge capital to start a business, then join a good network marketing company. It is not only a good passive income generator but you will also get personalized coaching in business, marketing and leadership skills from those who have stakes in your business.

So every night before you go to sleep calculate the number of hours you have spent in creating passive income for yourself as against the number of hours you have spent in generating linear income that has helped others get rich because of your effort. You must set a target each day to add more and more hours towards generating passive income. If you do this simple exercise on a regular basis you will take a giant leap towards attaining financial freedom.

1. Residual and Linear Income

To understand the difference between residual and linear income is critical to your financial wellbeing. Most people do not understand the distinction and stay in a job for their entire life or run a 'mom-and-pop' business that requires their attention and presence seven days a week.

So whenever you are looking at a business or an investment opportunity, look at the residual aspect. If it is not there then give it a miss. Never ever forget the commandment if you want to become truly rich: Thou shall work once and be paid for a lifetime.

The main problem with linear or earned income is that you are trading your time and skills for money. Your earning power will be limited by the time and skills you personally have. This is a very inefficient and arduous way of earning wealth. You have only 'X' number of hours in a day and also there is a limit to the skills you can acquire. These limiting factors will put a cap on your income.

As soon as you stop working or your skills become outdated your income will stop. You can take time out to upgrade your skills but during that period your income levels will either drop or stop altogether.

When it comes to linear income, you are the golden goose. As you grow older your physical and mental capacities get reduced. This will reflect directly on your earned income. In case of ill health or an accident your income will drop to a virtual zero.

Another major issue with earned income is that in virtually every country it is taxed more heavily when compared to investments or passive income. The biggest financial outflow in your life is the taxes. You pay virtually 40% to 70% of your earnings to the government in form of direct and indirect taxes. Some of the indirect taxes are invisible and you don't even come to know about them.

Linear or earned income has very limited number of loop holes to save on the taxes. If you are in a job you have to start investing or start a part time business to save on the taxes that will provide you with additional funds to build passive income for you and your family. This may seem unfair but it is true.

Most governments want you to invest your money so that capital formulation creates more jobs. This is why they give huge tax breaks to investors and business owners. You should take advantage of these tax breaks to create passive income for yourself.

If earned income have so many drawbacks then why most people seek jobs? The reasons are very simple. Jobs do not require a start-up capital or risk. Most people when starting out in life do not have capital and are risk averse.

The fault also lies in our education system which was designed during the industrial age to train people for jobs that the industries run by capitalists required. Things have changed dramatically with the advent of the information age. It is now possible to earn passive income with very little or virtually no start-up capital or risk.

There is no harm in starting up with a job because most of us start with linear income. The trick is to convert your linear income into passive income within the shortest period of time.

Can you become wealthy from earned income? It depends on your definition of wealth. Some professionals like doctors, investment bankers, lawyers and engineers are highly paid. But are they really rich or simply appearing to be rich? Do their jobs provide long term financial security? Can they sustain their life style if they lose their jobs for any reason?

The true secret of wealth is not that you have more money but that you have more time freedom. You do not have to trade your time for earning money. You will be rich when you can not only sustain your life style without working but also improve on it. In this case you have sufficient passive income to not only sustain your life style but also make your wealth grow by further investments into generating passive income.

When you are trading time for money you do not have time freedom. You can definitely become wealthy if you invest a part of your earned income into creating passive income which in course of time can surpass your earned income.

2. Passive Income Opportunities

Simply put passive income is an income that is not dependent on your time or effort. It is dependent on the asset and management of that asset. You have to leverage other people's time and money to create passive income and manage the asset.

Businesses can be a source of passive income only if you can replace yourself. If you are directly involved in your business on a day to day basis then it cannot be termed as a passive income. To turn your business into a passive income source you have to put the right kind of people and systems into place so that it operates without your presence and interference.

Most entrepreneurs start a business idea for them to generate millions but instead land up shackling themselves to their business and can't even afford to take a holiday in years.

The best kind of residual investments are those where you as the owner of the asset can exercise active control even though you are not involved in day to day operation. You must have adequate control over your asset so as to positively impact on the level of generated income.

Using other people's money and resources is the key ingredient of creating passive income. It buys you time and effort. Once you start creating passive income you will start attracting more and more of other people's money to grow even richer. If done correctly you will get caught in an upward spiral of residual wealth creation.

Passive income without doubt is the holy grail of investing and key to long term wealth. This is a critical step on your road to wealth creation. The earlier you begin this journey more is the success that you will achieve.

You can create a tidal wave in your financial security and prosperity if you do not waste a day. It is simple and easy. You simply have to make a start and there is no better time than today.

Passive income is important because every dollar you earn from this source is not dependent on your time or effort. Passive income gradually frees up your time to enhance creativity and improve quality of your life. It gives you financial security and improves your relationship with your family members as there are reduced time and finance constraints in your life.

Passive income frees up your time and also gives you tax breaks to give you even more dollars to create passive income. When you understand the residual game and implement it methodically, your income will spiral upwards along with freeing up your time.

You can never become rich on earned income because you are trading time for money. To become truly rich you have to separate your time from the money you earn. Creating wealth does not have to be about extracting last ounce of your energy. If you take a conscious decision you can gradually shift from linear income to generating passive income that will remain with you for generations to come.

Benefits of generating passive income:

- Freedom to choose when and where you wish to work

- Passive income is generated 24 hours 7 days a week

- Freedom to create unlimited amount of income only limited by your imagination

- Have time to spend with your family and friends or go on a vacation

- Retire young

- Financial security for your family in case of illness or ill health

- Ability to give to charitable causes dear to your heart

Before we discuss passive income opportunities, let me clarify the misunderstanding that has been created by the term 'passive income'.

From marketing point of view the term 'passive income' is very seductive as it equates to "No work", "No brainer", "Easy", "Just sit back and relax and money will come rolling in". People get excited and join a business opportunity thinking that there is no work involved. They get disillusioned when they find that the income is not passive after all.

Nothing can be further from truth. To create passive income there can be huge amount of time and effort upfront. There is no such thing as "100% passive income". Every income stream you create will require some effort up front and also some maintenance effort to sustain the passive income. You must keep these two work factors in mind before embarking on creating a passive income stream.

The good part is that once you have created your passive income stream then it will create a full time income for you with very few hours of work each week.

Now let us examine some of the passive income generating opportunities. You may use one or a combination of the methods to generate passive income.

Investors:

- Real Estate investors get cash flow from rent in addition to capital gain

- Saving Account owners earn interest

- Investors in shares get dividends and appreciation

- Discount mortgagers earn interest

- Tax lien certificate holders earn interest penalties

- Debenture holders earn interest businesses

Businesses

- Entrepreneurs who auto pilot their businesses earn passive profits

- Franchisors get a percentage of gross revenue or profits

- Partners get share of profits

- Venture partners get percentage of profits
  Authors get royalties from their books

Royalties:

- Musicians and song writers get royalties from their work

- Visual artists get royalties from paintings

- Inventors get royalties

- Game designers get royalties

- Actors get a percentage of the profits

Miscellaneous:

- Company Pension Plans offer income flow

- Retired persons get pensions

- Network marketers build passive income through leverage

- Corporate managers get stock options

- Insurance agents get passive income from their sales

- Securities agents get residual sales

- Celebrity endorsers get a gross percentage of profits

- Mailing list owners get rental fees

The above list is not exhaustive. It is possible to automate virtually any business by putting in systems and delegating authority. It is also possible to franchise businesses for passive income or sell shares to create wealth. There are always some costs involved. But the effort is worth it because what you will create is something more powerful. You will create income streams that do not need your presence.

The trick is let your money work for you and not you working for money. Once you start generating passive income your money will be working for you night and day even when you sleep.

3. Passive Income Categories

For clearer understanding we can divide passive income into two broad categories:

- Passive income sources that require startup capital or additional fund to maintain and grow

- Passive income sources that require little or no startup capital or maintenance money

The first category will need initial capital from your earned income, family money, funds from investors or borrowed funds from banks to purchase assets that will generate passive income for you. When you borrow money you create debt. This provides you leverage to create accelerated wealth but it also comes with associated risks that can destroy your wealth.

Examples of this type of passive income will be investing in stocks & other paper assets, real estate investments or buying businesses that have systems in place that need very little of your personal time to run the company. An example will be a good franchise business like the McDonalds that has systems in place and will need very little intervention on your part.

The second category of passive income requires very little financial out lay and is generated through assets that you create by writing a book, song, software, patent or trade mark. Internet has provided a new medium to generate residual wealth through creation of Virtual Real Estate.

Virtual Real Estate is the new gold rush and without doubt it is the new frontier that you have to master to create passive income. Internet is creating new millionaires every minute even as you read this book. What is virtual real estate? These are the assets you create on the internet. These include your websites, domain names, email lists, online businesses, Facebook, Twitter and other social media accounts. Once you create these assets you can generate passive income from them for years.

You can further categorize passive income into:

- Offline Passive income

- Online Passive income

Offline passive income generally requires more capital. You can take advantage of a variety of financial advisers and products to start investing in passive income investment schemes like paper assets and real estate. You can also get bank funding for buying these assets and hence can leverage your time and money.

On the other hand online passive income or creation of Virtual Real Estate requires very little and in some cases no start-up capital. There are many online gurus but no financial advisers. Banks will not fund it because the risks are too high. It is a new frontier of wealth creation that is still in progression.

It is still Wild West out there. You have to make the effort to increase your knowledge to create wealth in the new environment. Opportunities are endless. If you make the effort of mastering the new environment you can create large amounts of passive income with very little effort in shortest possible time frame.

Creating passive income on the internet does not give you financial leverage but technological leverage. Financial leverage creates debt with associated risks. Technological leverage on the other hand is debt free and faster.

The best instrument to be used to create passive income will depend upon your financial situation, time availability and state of knowledge at a given point. If you have plenty of capital and cash flow from your job or business but no time then it will be better for you to employ services of a professional financial adviser to invest in offline assets such as real estate, stocks, bonds, CDs, commodities like gold, silver etc.

On the other hand if you are internet savvy with little or no capital then creating Virtual Real Estate to generate passive income may be the right choice for you. You have to also take into account your risk appetite for a particular type of investment. Your assessment of your situation is the key to making a successful choice.

4. Getting Started

Let's be honest, starting is always the hardest part. It's chaotic; it's full of idealism, grandeur, and high expectations. Eventually, starting up usually ends with disappointment and frustration, so let's start somewhere different.

No high expectations, no idealism, and no chaos. Let's be smart and prudent about this, let's put our feet on the ground and take baby steps before we learn how to fly. After all, you do not need the additional stress.

The first thing that you need to understand when it comes to working for passive income is that you need to be doing this for a reason other than money. If you have a day job and you hate it, you are only going to make your life more miserable by finding a side job that you equally dislike. Why pile on the misery?

Ultimately, that means that you need to be doing this because you're truly interested about what it is you're deciding to supplement your income with. For example, if you decide that you're going to take a hack at eBook writing and you hate writing and reading, then you're destined to be a poor writer or author.

If you decided to invest in the financial markets such as stocks and bonds and you dislike looking at financial statements and stock charts, you are definitely not going to strike gold in the stock market.

Whatever you choose, it needs to be something that you're at least interested in and care about. For example, if you have a hobby that you want to turn into a lucrative source of income, that'll help you survive the initial rise of work.

Once money isn't your official desire and just a symptom of what you love, then you'll find truly find success happily. Dedicate yourself to spending the time to find the right niche for you, and invest the time and energy to become a master at it.

Passion will make the difference between everything. The detail to the work, the speed at which you accomplish your tasks and your ability to endure everything that's coming at you all depends upon whether you love what you do. So once more, be passionate and invested in what you're doing.

Secondly, it's vital that you're aware of how much work is going to be going into what it is you love. Do not for once think that this will be easy and that you'll only have to dedicate a small amount of time to it. That's why point number one with starting up is so important.

You've got to have the guts and the will to continue on when you only bring home ten bucks with your first eBook or you can't find a tenant for your property or no one wants to market through your blog or you only have a hundred people viewing your channel.

It's hard work and it's going to cost you a whole lot more in the beginning than you're making, but all great things in life take hard work and patience, so that leads to number three.

Stick with it! Endure and work and endure and work. That is what you're going to have to grind into your mind when you continue on this road. It's going to be exhausting and you're going to see only a meager reward (at first), but look on the bright side.

Draw your strength from the knowledge that even if you make a small amount of money to cover the labor and costs for starting up, know that it's more money than you had last time. Also, think about the productivity and the freedom you're getting in your personal life.

Fourthly, before you start up and take that first step, do your research. Look at how much this is going to cost you, look at what you need to be successful. If you're building a product, make sure that you're looking at the initial costs for everything you need to begin. Budget accordingly and be smart about what it is you're doing. This falls into the fifth step that I want to give you.

Have a plan! Once you're in the right mindset and you've put earnings on the backburner and have found exactly what you want to do with fiery passion, start budgeting for it and form a plan. Don't commit everything you have to this project at once.

Start out small, with a prototype of what you want to build. Whatever the project is, you need to start out small and test the waters. Once you've built, established, or designed a prototype of what you're interested in, start working on your next project.

Mark down how much time the prototype took and schedule the events needed to make it work. Continue with each project and monitor your progress. If you can look at the time you're spending on what, you can budget accordingly. It's a trick to keep you a float and in control, especially when you're in the beginning, which is arguably the most chaotic and insane part.

If you are thinking of going into investing, try to start out small before scaling up. Starting out small allows you to be more responsive to the market forces and be able to adapt more quickly. After all, if you fail, you will not lose everything.

Over the course of the book, I will introduce many ideas, which you can pick on to create your own passive income stream. Hopefully by the end of this book, you will have a solid fundamental understanding of what is possible and be able to embark on your very own journey towards passive income.

5. Passive Income Ideas

There are hundreds of ways in which you can create passive income. In this chapter we will discuss some offline business ideas that are easy to implement.

Rental properties

This is probably the most well known of all methods for obtaining monthly passive income. Real Estate has made more millionaires than any other asset class because frankly, it's fairly easy to grasp and even easier to invest in. If it's so easy, then why did so many people lose so much money during the crash?

Simply stated, people leaped into Real Estate investing without taking the time to learn a few basic principles. The main principle that they missed is that you make when you purchase a property; not when you sell it. But I'm getting ahead of myself, so let's start from the beginning.

A rental property is a piece of Real Estate that you rent out in order to receive a monthly income. The piece of property can be a single family home, a four-plex, an apartment complex, or even an entire shopping mall.

Just before the crash, people were purchasing rental properties with the knowledge that the monthly rental income wouldn't cover the mortgage, let alone the other expenses. They took a gamble that prices of homes would continue to rise, and obviously, they lost that bet. Now back to my original statement; you make money when you buy a rental property, not when you sell it.

Any time you are evaluating a potential rental property, make sure you crunch the numbers. Find out what the home price is, what it will rent out for, what taxes are, how much insurance is, how much HOA is (and what it includes if there is one), and other expenses. If a home can rent out for more than the sum of all the expenses (including a management fee, 10% maintenance expense, and 10% vacancy rate) and leave you a profit each month, then it's worth looking into the property further.

Rental income should cover all expenses and still put money into your pocket each month. If it does that, then the home price can go up, down, or stay the same. Either way the price fluctuates, you'll have your monthly income. That's why I said, you make money when you purchase a property. If it goes up in value, that's just an added bonus and should be viewed as such.

Buy an existing business

Most people think of long hours, no vacation, questionable pay, and an unknown future when the idea of owning a business comes to mind. To be fair, so does the idea of freedom and having no one to answer to. Most people dismiss this idea because it doesn't seem like passive income, but rather, a lot of hard work. But let's examine the idea a bit.

There's a difference between owning a business and owning a job that you think is your business. If your neighbor "owns" her own business but is stuck working 7 days a week for 10 hours each day, guess what? She owns a job... nothing more.

A true business owner collects businesses as if they were pieces of real estate, only using different evaluation methods. To put it another way, everyone knows that Donald Trump owns a few casinos, or has heard of a celebrity that owns a restaurant. But do you think that anyone ever sees Donald Trump dealing cards? Or do you think Puff Daddy ever washes dishes at his fine dining establishment?

The answer of course is no! These men and many other business owners rely on a trusted and skilled management team to run their businesses for them. Like rental properties, the cost of a good management team is built into the expected list of expenses. If a business's monthly income exceeds all of its expenses (including management!), then it may be worth further evaluation.

Starting a business from the ground up is a completely different animal all together. That is a full time job that pays very little, if anything at all. For the purposes of this book and for accumulating several cash flowing assets in the shortest period of time, we'll focus on existing businesses.

The cost for an existing business can vary from zero to billions. There is literally something at every price point. Jump online and just see what's available. Two great sites for buying small businesses are http://www.bizbuysell.com and www.businessesforsale.com

Look at businesses with low operational costs and that have as few employees as possible. Coin operated laundromats, automated carwashes, and storage facilities are all examples. The list of possibilities is endless.

This topic can fill volumes and this book is just meant to plant a few ideas and give some direction, so I'll only mention a few more things before moving on. Try to buy from people that have run their businesses successfully, have a great reputation, and are over the age of 50 and looking to retire.

If a person wants to retire, you can usually negotiate a better price. Also, try to keep them on as an employee for at least 6 months to a year. This way, your new management team can learn from the prior owner. More importantly, loyal customers can be introduced to, and warm up to, the new team while still seeing that familiar face.

There are also people who specialize in starting new companies so that they can flip them for a profit. Whatever route you decide, make sure you crunch the numbers and do your research!

Billboards

Billboards come in a variety of sizes, types, and prices. As with any real estate, the key to their value is location, location, location. The entry level billboard starts at about $25,000 and rent will range depending on the type, location, and demand.

Anything under $50,000 will typically be a very basic wooden billboard with a land lease. The next step up from there will be a single sided or double faced mono pole that seems to be common in a lot of cities. These can range anywhere from about $100K on up depending on location.

Top end billboards include digital advertising that rotates from one advertisement to the next. An inexpensive old model digital billboard can still start at $200K, but expect to be closer to the $400K mark. While this seems like a lot of money, marketing revenue from the billboard can easily add up to a lot of money as well.

Besides familiarizing yourself with the types of billboards, it is important to understand the difference between owning the land (typically commercially zoned), leasing land, and obtaining an easement.

Typically, people think that owning land would offer the best option, but this isn't always true. In the case of commercial real estate, not only can the cost of obtaining a piece of land be high, but taxes can be staggering as well. If you already own commercial property that is cash flowing and want supplemental income, that's when this option makes the most sense.

By far, the predominant method for placing a billboard involves some sort of land lease. This is a great option because instead of spending a ton of cash on commercial property on a busy road, an investor can typically sign a lease for a small fraction of what the billboard ad space will rent for.

Lease periods also tend to be 15+ years. It's a win-win for all involved. The landowner gets supplemental income for doing nothing except allowing you to use space that he or she probably wasn't even using, and you get a prime location for your billboard for pennies compared to what a land purchase would have cost you.

Option number 3 is by far the best of both. In a nut shell, easements allow you to occupy space that is owned by somebody else. In other words, instead of making lease payments, and having to renegotiate after 20 years, you pay one large fee up front for the right to put your billboard on someone else's land.

You never own the property, just the right to place your billboard there. Easements are generally seen a lot in neighborhoods in the form of fire hydrants, telephone poles, and utility service boxes. True, you own the land, but the city has an easement or right to put that stuff on your property. Just try to move it and see what happens (joking - do not do this!)!

Dividends

Dividends are a pretty obvious choice for anyone interested in purchasing paper assets. Dividends are generally a part of the profits that a publicly traded company shares or pays out to their owners, or shareholders. The beauty of dividends is that even if the stock price stays stagnant, you'll still profit off of holding shares because of those payouts.

Unfortunately, not all companies offer them. Typically larger companies tend to offer dividends. Blue-chip stocks are generally a good place to start looking. Look for companies with stable growth and a history of paying them out.

Dividends typically can vary from a half a percent, all the way up to 7%, with a lot of companies falling outside of that margin. While 7% doesn't sound like much, it's important to remember that banks are currently paying about 1% for money stored in your account. And that's if you're lucky! It's also important to remember that dividends are in addition to the added value if a stock goes up. So if a stock gains 10% for the year, and also paid out an additional 5% in dividends, that means you made a total of 15% from that stock! It also acts as a buffer when a stock goes down. Say a stock goes down by 10% but still pays out a 5% dividend. That means instead of losing 10%, your net loss is only 5%.

Obviously, picking stocks isn't as easy as I'm making it sound. Picking a great stock is an art form that has been mastered by very few individuals. Most professional mutual fund managers have a difficult time just keeping up with the S&P 500! So how are you supposed to pick the right stock? Research!

While no amount of research can guarantee that a stock continuously goes up, it can minimize the risk of it going down. Investing in stocks for dividend cash flow is like any other type of investment option mentioned in this book, in that it requires that you take the time to learn the way the game is played.

The best advice that I can give anyone is to invest on paper first for a few months. Just write your picks on a piece of paper and follow them. Once you have a little bit of confidence, start off with a small amount like $500. Open an account with an online company like www.scottrade.com or www.etrade.com

Once again, see how you do for several months before you increase the amount. If you're investing for dividends, remember that the goal is to find a good, stable company, with a history of paying dividends, and to hold the stock long term while the pay outs accrue. Think of it as a low paying annuity of sorts!

Selling covered calls

Now that you've found a great, stable company with a nice dividend payout of 5%, let's crank up the cash flow. Stock options have a reputation for being extremely volatile and risky... and they can be. But they can also be a lot safer than a stock by itself as well. First, let's talk about the basics of what options are.

Options are the right to buy or sell a specified stock at a given price (called the strike price) by an expiration date. The right to buy a stock is called a "call." The right to sell is called a "put." There is also "naked" versus "covered." Selling a "naked call" means that you do not own the stock.

Selling a "covered call" means that you do own the stock. If this all seems confusing, re-read the paragraph a couple times and write it out if you have to. To help you further understand what these are, let's go over some examples.

Example 1) John wants to buy stock in company at $10 per share. He thinks it will go up, but it all hinges on their quarterly earnings. If earnings are bad, the stock can plummet. John buys 100 shares at $10 apiece for a total of $1000. John also decides to buy a "put" option.

He buys one contract (options are sold by the contract; one contract consists of 100 shares) for

$100 that has a strike price of $9 per share and expires in 60 days. The "put" option acts like an insurance policy in this case. If John is right and the stock hits $15 per share, he loses the money he paid for the option but still comes ahead by $4 per share ($5 per share increase - $1 per share for the "put").

If the stock plummets to $4 per share though, John's "put" option would allow him to still sell that stock for $9 per share. Remember, a "put" is the right to sell at a given price by a certain date. John would limit his losses to $2 per share instead of $6 per share, which means that the option was actually less risky than owning just the stock in this case. Why would he loose $2 per share? $9 sales price per share - $10 purchase price per share - $1 "put" price = -$2.

Example 2) John wants to buy shares in a company that are priced at $100 per share. The company is expecting to announce huge profits for the quarter. John only has $1000 and would like to control more than just 10 shares.

Instead of buying 10 shares, he can buy a "call" option with a strike price of $110 and an expiration of 60 days. The option costs $1000. With the call option, John would have the option to buy the stock at $110 per share even if it hits $150 per share within the 60 day period (options can last for days or for years depending on what your preference is).

Now let's look at the difference between owning the stock verses the call option in terms of potential profit. If John had 10 shares, and the stock did hit $150 per share, he would make a profit of $50 per share or a total of $500. Not too bad, but let's look at the kind of leverage that the "call" option offers.

If he still paid $1000 but controlled 100 shares, those 100 shares would have gone up by $4000! His call option gave him the right to buy 100 shares of the stock at $110 per share (one contract) or a total of $11,000 worth of stock. If it goes to $150 per share (or $15,000 worth of stock), he can exercise his option to buy the stocks at the strike price of $110 per share, sell the stocks at the $150 per share price and keep the difference of $4,000.

His actual profit would be $3,000 because the option cost him $1,000, and there would be transaction fees, but he would just about triple his money. The stock could of course never go above $110 per share though, in which case John would lose his entire $1,000. This would obviously be an example of how risky options can be.

How do we get cash flow from all of this? Simply put, by selling long shot covered calls on the stocks that we purchased for our dividend investment. The two examples were of John buying options. But who is he buying the options from? Other investors! Selling puts can be likened to selling insurance policies, and can be risky. We're going to be selling "covered calls" which are relatively safe when compared to other investment options.

Assuming you took my advice and purchased a stable company without a lot of volatility, you can now sell other investors a call option to buy your 100 shares of stock at a higher price than it is currently at. Say you purchased a stock at $6 per share and are enjoying a dividend of 2%, but want more from it.

You can sell someone else an option to purchase your 100 shares for the predetermined price of $8 per share and a 6 month expiration date. For that privilege, they will pay you $30 for the contract (100 shares). If you do that every 6 months or twice a year, that's an additional 10% on top of your 2% dividend!

What happens if the price goes above the strike price of $8? Then they may execute the option and you'll have to sell your shares at $8 per share (plus you get to keep all the money you made from selling the options). Keep in mind; if you purchased the stock at $6 per share, you're still making a great profit!

Finance properties

Real estate can be a very good passive income but it's not just because of the amount of leverage or the amount of tax breaks that exist; it's also because of the amount of options that exist! We're going to talk about two of them in this section. Both involve acting as though you are the bank.

If you have a large amount of cash sitting around, this option may be for you. Right now bank loans are difficult to obtain for many people. As a result of this and of the 2006-2007 housing crash, houses are at some of their lowest prices in years.

This option calls for purchasing a foreclosure at a rock-bottom price, raising the price by 10 to 20%, then selling it by offering low money down, and low qualification owner financing. You can than charge a higher interest rate over the banks because of the extra risk you are taking on. You're making money by both selling at a higher price and by financing at a high interest rate. Why would somebody buy your house at a higher price and a high interest rate? It may be their only option because they had a foreclosure in their past.

Also, if you got a great deal on a foreclosure, your new price may be at or near the current market value and not seem all that inflated. The nice thing is that there's a ton of people looking to buy a home that can't get bank financing, so you have a huge pool of people to sell to.

But even if you pick someone who is sub-par and they stop paying their mortgage, you can foreclose of them and try again! Let me say that in another way, if they stop paying, you get to keep the house plus all the money they already paid you! You can be as selective as you want when choosing who to sell to, and you should pick the best applicant.

You in essence become the bank and receive monthly mortgage payments. Another nice thing is that there are companies that specialize in collecting the mortgage payments for you, making sure the tax and insurance is paid, and collecting late payments. Their service charge is cheap too. Find out who your local mortgage servicing company is by contacting a local escrow company. They can usually refer you to one.

So you don't have $100K sitting around? There's another way to "become the bank." You can either use a wrap around loan or a "lease to own" program. A wrap around loan involves obtaining a conventional loan at a bank, then selling the house at the higher price and interest rate.

You then use the mortgage servicing company to collect payments, pay your mortgage, the property taxes, and the insurance, and then send you the difference. Generally speaking, when you transfer the title to your home, it triggers a payoff clause in your contract with the mortgage lender.

The way around this is to write up a sales contract with your new buyer and to hold off on transferring the title. The actual title transfer can take place after the new owner improves their credit and refinances the property with a bank loan, or when they pay off the property. Their interest in the property will be protected by the contract that is written up.

Another way to "become the bank" is to offer a lease-to-own option. In this scenario, you offer the house at a fair market price or slightly above, and at a high rental rate with a portion of the rental income going towards the down payment of the home.

If renters choose to move forward with the purchase at the end of the contract, you then use the extra money as their down payment, or portion of their down payment and have them either precede with a conventional bank loan if they qualify, or precede with a wrap around loan.

Vending route

Admittedly, this method does require a bit of work, but depending on the machines you choose, the amount of time can be minimized considerably. Also, if you have teenagers in your house that are in need of work, managing your vending route can be a great job for them and free you up to explore other opportunities.

Cash flow potential from your vending route will depend on several factors including location, the type of machine, the demand for the product offered, whether it has a marketing revenue option, how many machines you have, and whether it accepts cash and/or credit. Let's take a closer look at all of this.

First, your location needs to have as much foot traffic as possible. While this may sound obvious, you'd be surprised where I have seen some machine placement! Free areas are rarely best. Figure out who your target market is and scout different areas where your market is likely to frequent. If there are machines already, do they offer what yours does? Talk to the owner of the business or property. Would they be open to letting you place one of your machines there for a percentage of the profits? What is a fair percentage?

Check online and ask around about what is typical for your area. Some prime locations include colleges, universities, malls, hospitals, large companies, bars, and food stores. The location will also depend on what your offering and if there's a demand for that product in your chosen area. For example, a "live lobster crane" machine probably won't fly in an office building, but a sandwich machine might!

"Live Lobster Crane" machine; yes, they exist! So do a whole host of other machines that range from dispensing money (ATM's), to electronics, soda, sandwiches, candy, ice cream, DVD rentals, and more. If it doesn't exist, then have one made! Be creative. You're only limited by your imagination with this one. It is with that said that I will remind you of our goal; income with little to no work.

Coin counting machines offer people the option of dropping in all of the coins that they've been saving in exchange for bills... for a price of course! One of the least expensive machines out (prices range from a couple hundred for a gumball dispenser to $20K for a DVD kiosk) is an automated breathalyzer for bars.

They can start off for around $1000 and require very little maintenance (a few straws and re-calibration every other week at most). Some of them offer another added benefit: marketing revenue.

Some machines offer the added benefit of having side plates and/or LCD screens that allow you to sell advertisement space to local businesses. Often times, the marketing revenue can out pace vending sales! And if you get enough machines, you may be able to get a local marketing company to sell the ad space for you.

This brings us to our last couple of points. Obviously, more machines can mean more revenue, but start off small. Try it out with just a couple of machines and see how it goes; what locations work, and which don't; what sells and what doesn't. As far as credit card vs. cash, the debate is ongoing. Anytime your machine accepts cash, it becomes a target for vandalism.

Of course if you don't accept cash, you're limiting your market to those with a credit card. It will ultimately be up to you to decide and to weigh the pros and cons of all the options. My advice is to talk to the vending company your buying from and see what they have to say. How much does it cost for repairs? Is there a warranty?

What does it cover and for how long? Remember to research any investment that you're pursuing!

Tax liens

If you've ever been up late at night watching TV, then you've probably seen an infomercial or two about tax liens. I'm going to let you in on a little secret; you don't need an infomercial's how-to program to invest in tax liens. And for the record, they are great to invest in!

It always pays to ask. The people working in the treasurer's office can be a gold mine of information! The county treasurer's website can also provide a ton of information.

The way that tax liens work is simple. The local government needs your property taxes to operate (to pay politicians, cops, politicians, teachers, politicians, pay for street repairs, etc.). If a person doesn't pay their property taxes by the due date, there's usually a penalty and/or high interest rate added onto their tax bill.

The government uses this as an incentive to get people to pay on time. Here's where it gets good. Being that our government likes to live paycheck to paycheck, they prefer to get their money (really, your money) immediately and they don't necessarily care for the interest or penalty accrued.

So they let normal citizens put up the money for the taxes owed and in exchange, give the investor a "tax lien" against the property that is being taxed. Tax liens can be for just about any piece of real estate. When the owner of the property finally pays their tax bill, the holder of the lien not only gets their money back, but the government lets them keep all of the accrued penalties and/or interest!

Interest rates and penalties run anywhere from 6% to 300%! How do you get 300%? In Texas, if a person is even 1 day late with their taxes, they are hit with a 25% penalty. 25% in one month is roughly equal to an annual interest rate of 300% (25% x 12 months = 300%). Most states pay between 10% and 20%.

What happens if someone doesn't pay their taxes? In some states, if a person doesn't pay off their tax lien within 3 years, the lien holder can foreclose on the property. Being that a tax lien is a first lien; all other liens including mortgages are wiped out. A government lien trumps most other liens. Every state is different though.

Some let you foreclose, others auction off the property in order for you to get your money (Florida is one example). You'll have to look into your individual state to find out if you can foreclose, how much the interest rate or penalty is, and how to obtain liens. Some states have investors bid the interest rate down at a tax lien auction, others sell the liens over-the-counter, and others differ from county to county.

A few final tips; always physically go to see the property. Also, look for farm land. It's valuable, taxes are cheap (because it's highly subsidized), and often times farmers own it outright. Anything with a mortgage is tough to foreclose on because banks will usually step in and pay off the tax lien, and then charge it back to the home owners. Are they really that nice? No, they are just protecting their interest. Remember, a government lien (a tax lien) wipes out all other liens if you foreclose on a property.

Tax liens take some research, but once you buy a bunch, you can sit back and enjoy the stream of checks you get as people pay off their taxes.

Mineral rights

Do you currently own a piece of land that you think is either worthless or can't cash flow? The next few methods center on vacant land and how to make it work for you. Admittedly, the options are less common, but that doesn't mean impossible.

The first method involves leasing out the mineral rights (which include natural gas, oil, or precious metals rights) to a mining company. But first you'll have to look into whether or not you own the rights or not. Believe it or not, the government often times retains ownership of any valuable resources that can be extracted from the land you think you own.

That doesn't mean you can't obtain the rights from them, it just means that it's an extra step in an already drawn out process. But before you even do that, you'll want to look into whether or not mining companies are even in that area, and if so, what they are mining. If there are companies in the area, that's a good sign, but your research is still far from over.

Your next step will be to contact someone to do a geological survey to see if your land has potential. If it does, then you can either hire someone to obtain samples and measurements (very expensive), or contact local mining companies. If they are already in the area, they may be willing to handle the exploration and sampling.

Land for rent

You do not have to limit renting your lot to just RV owners. Can it be used as farm land? What about an automated parking lot? How about for long term car storage? Contact local bus companies to see if you can work out a deal. Try to think outside of the box. The trick is to try to keep it as inexpensive as possible to get it rent ready. At the very least, try putting a for-rent sign on your lot and see what offers come in. You never know what ideas other people will come up with. Make sure you are familiar with what the property is zoned for before moving forward with any deal!

Drop shipping

You don't have to drive around long before you see a bunch of closed businesses. Much of it is due to a poor economy, but some of it is also due to competition from online businesses. Online retail stores offer many advantages (to both owners and consumers) over traditional "brick and mortar" shops such as convenience, lower prices, larger selection, product reviews, little to no employees, no inventory, no theft of merchandise, and in some cases, no sales tax.

One just needs to look at the property taxes that our government charges on commercial real estate to know that the odds are stacked against "brick and mortar" retail shops. But how do online retail stores work? One way is by "drop shipping."

Drop shipping is a supply chain management technique which eliminates the need for physical retail space. Your primary job as the online business owner is to maintain a website that offers several products. You'll also be handling customer care as well.

As customers order products, the orders get forwarded to your wholesale supplier who then ships the product directly to the customer. The nice thing is that the business owner gets to set the price and keep the difference between retail and wholesale pricing.

Example: John orders x from your site and pays your price of $100. Wholesale supplier #1 ships product x to John and charges you the wholesale price of $60. You get to keep the difference of $40.

Drop shipping allows retail store owners to sell a wide variety of merchandise in a virtual store without ever having to hold any inventory. Online stores offer anything from food to adult toys and everything in between. Since the store is online, no physical retail space is needed, just a web address and a host for it.

Another thing that you will need to set up is a shopping cart, or the ability to accept payments from your customers. PayPal offers a button that you can plug to your site, and it works well for simple transactions. Stand-alone carts that keep the customers on your webpage can be set up through sources like http://www.candypress.com or http://www.zen-cart.com

It's best to hire someone to help with the set up as it can get confusing. There's a ton of people who offer website design services at competitive pricing.

How do you find a wholesale supplier? There are a myriad of wholesalers to choose from. A great site for finding a wholesaler is www.worldwidebrands.com. They charge a bit, but offer a life time membership and have the best database for finding suppliers.

Online retail stores that are already up and running can also be purchased on websites like eBay as well. The best advice that I can give is to educate yourself on drop shipping before jumping in.

It sounds easy! What's the catch? One word: marketing. Most online stores fail because they simply can't drive enough people to their website. If you decide to proceed with this method, you will want to market through various social media sites such as Facebook and Twitter. You'll also want to use Google AdWords.

The way this works is that links to your site are posted on other websites, and every time someone clicks on your link, you pay the owner of that website anywhere from $0.01 to $0.10. The link acts as a virtual billboard and the price you pay per click is the incentive for sites to host your link.

The nice thing is that you can set a limit regarding how much you want to spend. Google actually does a great job of giving you complete control.

Thorough marketing cannot be completed without search engine optimization or SEO. SEO is basically the process of getting your link to show up on the first page or two of a given search engine anytime someone searches your selected key words. Large companies spend vast fortunes keeping their companies at the top of the searches, and SEO services can get very expensive. Luckily, it's a skill that can be learned.

Drop shipping and marketing are two topics that can fill volumes. With that said, this method of passive income will take a good amount of time to learn, but once up and running, should take less and less time as you learn the ropes.

Hobbies

Do you love building model cars, fixing real cars, building furniture from raw wood, or making homemade soaps, why not make money doing the things you love? There are plenty of hobbies out there that will make you money because there's a demand for it.

For example, I knew a guy who was obsessed with model trains. I thought it was the most stupid hobby in the world and that man spent a ridiculous amount of money buying unique train sets to build, paint, and craft a whole world for them to be displayed on. I called it a waste of time, stupid, nerdy, and completely moronic.

Well, little did I know that this guy was pulling in thousands of dollars every month for his late night, winding down relaxation hobby! Seriously, Thousands of dollars! This man was part of an elaborate online community and fulfilling a need that was desired. And this isn't exclusive for model trains.

Do you have any idea how much it costs to build a chair after initial costs? Lumber is cheap and a handcrafted, expertly assembled chair with a beautiful and trusted finish will run over three hundred dollars, more depending upon the wood that you use. And let me tell you, all you have to do is invest the time learning this hobby. And there's a huge market everywhere for something like furniture.

The point is that any hobby that you decide to pick up will have a market for someone wanting to buy a finished product that's handmade. I just met a guy who sells origami sculptures that he's made and ships them overseas to people wanting unique origami figures.

Now, this again, will require marketing and education if you currently don't have a hobby that's worth any money. But, learning a hobby that's worth the time and money mastering, is worth it regardless of whether or not you're making money at it.

Every person alive should have a hobby that they've invested themselves into and if you have that, you can also make money from it. This is a simple trade to get into, because it's entirely motivated by you. Take the time, say a year, and really get into it.

Start mastering the craft that you love, learn about it as much as you can, and take some classes that you can. Once you've mastered or gotten a handle on your trade, start selling off your pieces.

You can employ the Internet to help garner interest, social networking, and even a physical presence in flea markets or local tradeshows will really boost your accessibility to your clients. You just have to work hard to get those people interested.

If you are really into handicrafts, a great platform I'd recommend is Etsy. Etsy is a platform for people to buy and sale high quality or vintage items. The item range has an impressive assortment including craftsmanship, photography, garments, ornaments, foods, antique items, sewing products, toys, and numerous other unique items. Etsy's mission is to enable everyone to make a living, making the things they love, and to connect makers with buyers from around the world.

Now, the drawbacks for this might start with you not having a hobby that will make you money. If that's the case, you're going to need learn a hobby and that will take you time. Of course, you'll need to invest the time to overcome that.

Also, you're going to need to invest money in what you'll be required to have to start this project. These are minor if you're really investing in something that you love.

Secondly, a hobby might not necessarily mean passive income becomes you are still trading your time for money. However, as your business grows and scales up, you will be able to charge more for you products and this translates to a higher dollar value per hour of effort you put in. If you want to start a crafting business, I wish you all the best!

6. Online Passive Income Ideas

The reason why you must start building passive income using internet is because it is revolutionizing the way we think, work and shop.

- It is the most Powerful Media much bigger than television

- It is the Biggest Market Place

- It is the Most Profitable Business

- It is Getting Bigger Every Day

- Internet Business Never Stops 24 hours 365 days

- Requires Very Little Investment and hence No Risk

- It has created more Millionaires and Billionaires than any other opportunity

- It is for Everyone

- You can automate your business very easily to create passive income

There was over $300,000,000,000 in sale over the internet last year. This figure is growing exponentially each and every year. Even if you are able to capture 1/1,000,000 part of this business your earnings will $300,000 per year. How many shares are you prepared to capture?

Once you build your build your internet income it will provide you with passive income and freedom of time to travel the world in style, meet people and share your ideas.

There are hundreds of ways to make money on the Internet. Your aim is to find a business that can be automated easily.

Some of the methods you can use are:

Affiliate marketing

This is passive income derived from setting up a blog or website that pre sells a company's products. You provide reviews and information that drives traffic to your affiliate link. You get paid by the company if someone buys the product from your affiliate link.

The trick is to find products that are not only popular but pay good re-occurring commissions. This will create a monthly passive income for you once a sale is made. One such example is selling a monthly subscription to a membership site. Also find products that pay multi-tier commissions. You will then get paid if your affiliate makes a sale.

You must also look at the sales page of the product you are promoting. If the sales page of the product you are promoting is not a good one then your conversion rate will be poor. This means that if you refer 1000 visitors to a sales page through pre-selling on your website and only a handful convert then your effort will be in vain. If a sales page converts well then you will make more money for the same amount of effort.

Say you're already into the blogging world or you have an extensive presence online with your own website. Want to still make more money with that hobby of yours? Then why not invest a little time and research into affiliate marketing?

Of course, there's that huge prerequisite with this one. You need to have a website with **A LOT** of traffic. I put that in fantastic, bold letters so you'll really focus on it. Why is that important with this? Well, let's start out by discussing what it is.

So, affiliate marketing is when companies pay you for advertising on your website, which leads to sales on their website. So if you have a blog that is bringing in hundreds of people every day and a company that sells spoons wants to advertise on your website, every click on the banner ad they put up on your website, which leads to a sale, puts money in your pocket. This is truly passive income at its finest. You do absolutely nothing but keep on getting people to your website, which is what you want in the first place, right? So affiliate marketing is probably what I'm going to have in this book that is the most genuine example of passive income. However, I like to coin it as 'symbiotic income' because it goes hand in hand with work that you're already doing.

This of course, isn't exclusive to websites or blogs. In fact, companies will pay you to get decals on your car to advertise for their company. It's everywhere, but the most common form you'll find is on blogs and websites. If you are into blogging or you've taken the step into the eBook market, you'll definitely want to consider combining eBook writing and affiliate marketing for a double combo of income.

Now, back to my original question, why do you need an established website or blog before you start this? Well, the answer is simple. If your income from affiliate marketing is dependent upon people clicking on that ad on your website, then you need to play the numbers game.

If one out of twenty people click on that advertisement and make a purchase, then you want to get two thousand people coming into your website just so you can make a steady, decent income. After all, we're not doing this for nickels and dimes, are we?

So, if you're starting from the ground up with this and having affiliate marketing as your primary goal, then you're going to want to reconsider, just this once, if it's doable. If you think you can generate that kind of traffic with a new idea, then get to work.

Generating traffic to a website takes effort and there are people who specialize in Search Engine Optimization which directs traffic to websites. If you are new in this field, you will find that the competition is tough.

With the exponential growth of social media, it is sometimes even possible to carry out affiliate marketing by promoting products on Twitter or Facebook. This has made the barrier to entry to affiliate marketing even lower. If you would like to be an affiliate marketer, a great resource I'd recommend is going to Clickbank.com. This is a great platform for affiliate marketers to choose the product they want to promote and they also offer concise and detailed resources on how to help a marketer get started.

Now, obviously, there are going to be drawbacks with this form of passive income. It is entirely dependent upon website traffic and the demand of the product. For example, if you're doing a food blog, you don't want to advertise tires. You want to have an affiliate who is selling kitchen equipment, food, or something like that. So if the ads are inappropriate for your market, then it's going to be difficult.

The second drawback is that you're dependent upon your readers to actually click on the banner and buy the product. Increasing your readership can compensate this. If you already have an established fan base, this is just a great way to make a little extra cash.

The last disadvantage of going into affiliate marketing is actually the amount of effort that is required to make a substantial income is you don't have an established website or follower base. You have to spend a lot of time trying to identify the next hot trend and find the next hot product to promote so that you can earn the most money. It is a consistent cat and mouse game that you are playing where you are always chasing the next big thing.

I have personally a few of my friends getting completely burnt out by the long hours they have to put in to make this a successful business. To overcome this, I'll go back to my previous point, which is to build a loyal following and always provide them with quality content. It will help a great deal if you are curating content, which you personally can relate to and are interested in. This will keep you motivated!

Information products

People search the internet to find information or solution to their problems. They may be looking for information on weather, health issues, travel information, holiday destinations, cheap tickets, relationship problems, how to make money or how to fix a problem.

Human appetite for information is limitless. They also come on the internet for socializing, fun and recreation. You can create information products to satisfy these needs. You can create a report or an eBook to help them solve their problem and sell it on the internet.

So what does it take to be an eBook writer?

Well, let me tell you. It takes endurance. It takes having an adaptive personality, and it takes quantity. The key to succeeding as an eBook writer is being able to get a lot of product out to the public and working with a massive network. You're only going to succeed if you know how to set up a fan base and get a lot of books out to them. So how do you start?

Starting out entirely depends upon what you're able to put out and to figure that out, you need to turn to your plan. Firstly, find out what are you going to write. The eBook market is no longer a gold rush in which any person can just grab a keyboard, type away and make some money.

You will need to carry out proper research on the topic you want to write and also produce a great piece of work. A great way to find out the hot topics is by going into Amazon Kindle store and look for the top bestsellers. In the bestseller's list, you will discover a list of books that are taking the readers by storm. These are the books that resonate with the readers and it might pay to look into these genres.

For example, Twilight is an international best seller; it probably pays to write a series of fiction title that is related to vampires and werewolves. Perhaps there is a book that is currently selling well in the weight loss market, and therefore, you might want to create a few books that explore that niche.

Next, you want to figure out how much you can write. List all the topics that you want to write. From this list, you have to decide if you are a non-fiction or fiction author. Once you've decided what you're going to write and have listed out how many books you're going to be able to write at this moment, you can start to map out those books.

Many authors often overlook outlining. I cannot stress enough the importance of outlining because they connect your chain of thoughts. During the outlining phase, you want to regurgitate everything you know about the subject as well as all any research you
have done on the topic onto a blank screen or paper.

Once this process is done, you can arrange what you have written into chapters and in chronological order. If the structure of the book looks good, you may proceed with the writing. Write whenever you get a chance.

It's important for you to have quantity with eBooks. You need to have a lot to write about in order to make money through this route. But having the books is not going to be enough. Simply uploading to major websites, such as Amazon, who is responsible for over 70% of eBook sales, or Smashwords, isn't going to be enough for you to get the money that you might be seeking. If all you've done is uploaded eBooks and leave them there, then you're going to be disappointed.

You need marketing and networking, which means you will need to build a blog, a website, and a presence on every social networking website. You may even create a YouTube channel to promote your books if you wish. The lie about self-publishing is that you don't need publishing houses.

The truth is that publishing houses provides important marketing and distribution, which means that you're going to need to pickup that end of the work as well. So once you've written your books, start getting in touch with your readers to boost your sales.

The best thing you can do is to build an email list. At the end of every book, insert a link that directs the readers to a form that collects their email addresses. To entice readers to do this, offer a free product, which will only be given to them if they sign up to your email list.

Why create an email list? An email list is a power contact list, which shares insight with you on your target audience. Suppose you are going to release another book in the same genre in the future, you can tap on this list to market your book! You are also able to create personal relationships with your readers through this channel.

Yes, it is a lot of work, but you need to put the effort into it for this to be a lucrative means to passive income. If you're willing to put the time and the energy into your work, then you'll get to the point where you're making steady income here.

I know several people who make 8,000 to 10,000 dollars monthly just from their eBooks, but it's taken a lot of work. Once you get to that point, here's the secret you're not expecting. You're going to have to keep it up. You'll need to keep writing, but in the end, you'll have fans writing you and encouraging you to continue on. You'll love it.

The drawbacks here however, are the facts that you're going to need to really work with this one. It's a lot of work that's going to need to go into this endeavor and you're not going to find a lot of income being generated for years to come.

You also need to come to terms with the fact that not every book you write is a going to be a hot seller. Some books simply do not sell as well as the rest because of various reasons and you must not be disheartened by these perceived failures. If you have the patience, the time, and the dedication to do this job, then I would suggest you get out there and carve out a little piece of it yourself!

Software products

You don't have to be a software engineer to create a software product. All you need is a great idea of what people want to do faster and easier.

The best example is Bill Gates who created the Windows Operating System. Everyone who has a PC needs it. You could do the same on a smaller scale.

Once you have an idea you can go to a software developer to develop that product for you. If you don't know any software engineer to execute the job then you can go to elance.com or upwork.com and post your requirement. Software developers will give their quotes and you can hire one of them after determining their credentials.

You get paid to solve the problems. The bigger the problem your software can solve more you can charge the people. Start by solving small problems and then graduate into developing software for more complex problems.

If you look into your daily life you will be able to analyze what functions you need to automate to reduce your workload. You can develop software to automate those functions and market it. But before you start developing a software check in the market place if such software with the functions you need is available otherwise you will be re-inventing the wheel.

Creating software will not give you a passive income. You will have to learn the skill to market the software. Clickbank is a great place to start because it is a market place where you can recruit hundreds if not thousands of affiliates to promote your software product on profit sharing basis.

Advertising income

You can generate residual advertising income from your website if you have organic traffic coming from search engines. You can offer advertising or banner space to various advertisers for a fee or revenue sharing.

The trick here is to create a niche website with great content and build backlinks so that search engines not only find your website but also rank you high in the search engines. This will drive traffic to your website. Your passive income will increase in direct proportion of the traffic to your website.

Create a membership site

You can create a membership site and charge a monthly membership fee for accessing information on your website if you are an expert in a field. People will pay for your knowledge, resources you offer and the support you provide. The more members you gain the more passive income you make.

You can increase membership of your site by offering an affiliate program wherein you share your monthly revenue with people who bring in new members to your site.

Because you are an expert in your field, you can also recommend other affiliate products and services to your members, from which you earn commissions.

YouTube and podcasts

Starting podcasts and YouTube channels can be a form of passive income as well. As with any other businesses, to starting making substantial money from it, you will need the critical mass of audience that religiously follow what you are doing. Once you have that group of followers, there are many channels, which you can adopt to make money.

You can do affiliate marketing and sell products that you endorse to your followers, or you can slap on advertisements in your podcast or YouTube videos to earn money from the impressions created by views or downloads of your work. I've personally heard of people who earn upwards of $100,000 per month just from running a successful YouTube channel. Yes, you read that right. $100,000 a month. Of course, that is not to say that everyone can achieve it by creating a random video of a cat playing piano. You have to understand your audience and POTENTIAL audience and regularly produce content that resonates with them.

When you look at the prospect of starting a podcast, or a channel on YouTube, it's pretty tantalizing because they all have one thing in common. They're cheap. That's right, super dirt-cheap. And that's the one of the major benefit that I'm going to focus on for you.

When beginning a Podcast or YouTube channel, you need to realize that all of these require an Internet connection and a computer strong enough to do what you're interested in. That being said, those are pretty much the only financial costs that you need for startup materials. Most of us have both of those things, so that makes the beginning of this project extremely simple.

The important thing to invest in is the material and this investment is non-trivial. Not physical materials, but in actual content that is engaging and going to make people want to participate in what you have to offer. Remember, most of these projects are still in the Wild West phase where pretty much everything goes and there's still a lot of unexplored territory that you can carve a piece from or usurp the leading personalities.

For a Podcast, you're going to need a topic or source to draw from. Do something that you're passionate about and that there's plenty of material. Don't limit yourself. Say you sell real estate and you want to do a fun, engaging real estate podcast. Well, don't just limit it to high-end studio apartments in downtown locations. You'll run out of material within weeks. Do something broad and with plenty of minor topics. Again, invest in that initial plan to see what you can come up with.

The next thing you're going to want to do is invest in a microphone that's going to make you sound legitimate. Don't kill your listeners with terrible audio. Learn to soundproof your room and find someone else that you can banter with on the show. People get tired of listening to just one voice, but two or a panel of people, that's engaging. They'll feel like part of the crew.

Lastly, don't be afraid to expand or take endorsement opportunities. For example, if you're doing a real estate podcast, see if other realtors will pay for a shout out or a chance to be interviewed and share their experience. It'll work.

If you are running a podcast for the online audience, don't be afraid to provide endorsement for digital products or membership websites. I would recommend that you only promote the product, which directly benefits your listeners. The last thing you need is turning away a few angry listeners and getting a bad reputation all because of promoting one bad, lousy product.

Finally, a YouTube channel is a quick way to get money through advertisement and views on YouTube. Again, the crucial point to a YouTube channel is to have content that is engaging and fun for the viewer. If you're not going to be able to provide that kind of an experience, garnering views is going to be hard. So take the time to sit down and plan out what it is you're going to do. If you have friends that are interested in the idea, get them involved.

So of these digital opportunities, there are plenty of drawbacks. What if people don't like what you have? What if you bomb? What if you can't get people hooked? Well, pretty much every drawback that comes with these cheap opportunities can be overcome with three words: trial and error. Keep tinkering and figure out what works.

Rarely does someone hit the jackpot on his first try. The same can be said with building a YouTube channel or podcast. Some of the most famous "YouTubers" and "Podcasters" started out with no more than 100 religious followers. In fact, 100 followers are all you need to be successful. The reason is because you can better manage your relationships with your followers when the group is not large. This personal touch will add to the stickiness factor and turn these followers into advocates for your brand and business.

In a nutshell, you'll be able to get what you want and get people excited for your product if you just stick with it and stay motivated.

It takes time and effort to master this medium but once you get it right, there is minimum amount of effort involved in generating passive income of your dreams. The trick is to master one strategy properly and it can provide you with passive income to retire.

Most people fail because they tend to lose focus and jump from one opportunity to another. When it comes to the internet one can get distracted easily because it has so much to offer in terms of information, entertainment and social interaction.

I have discussed various passive income opportunities but nothing will come of them if you don't take action. You have to do independent research based on your knowledge and passion. Find a business that is best suited to your temperament and situation.

You can convert your knowledge and passion into dollars. Don't fake it be real. Each one of us is born with some unique talent and we experience life in a manner that is also unique to us. We have to share this unique experience with others to earn money on the internet.

Next you must find a business model to share your unique knowledge, talent and experience. Because we are interested in generating passive income, focus on a business opportunity that can be automated. Buy the best product that teaches you the technique. Then simply focus and don't stop till the money starts to flow in.

7. Multiply Your Passive Income Streams

The rich people do not depend on only one source of income, but grow orchards of "money trees."

The famous Nile is the longest river on planet earth. If you look down from a space craft orbiting the earth you will be able see it and its 2 main tributaries quite clearly. It is that big and long. But what you can't see from outer space is all of the thousands of little streams and rivers that run into the Nile. It is all that water from thousands of small streams that pour into the Nile making it so large and invincible.

If you examine the rich, you will find that their income is like the river Nile. They have several streams of income pouring in from different sources to create a huge cash flow of residual wealth.

The primary benefit to multiple streams of income is the consistency and security of your income coming from non-related sources.

Every product or business has what's known as a "Product Life Cycle." Each and every product or business goes through the following four phases:

- Market introduction stage

- Growth stage

- Maturity stage

- Saturation and decline stage

What effect this has on your effort to create passive income? Your passive income source is either growing or dying. Some passive income steams will last through your lifetime but some may dry up pre-maturely. It is great to enjoy the benefits of a passive income stream for the period it lasts. But eventually outside factors will decrease the profits.

Eventually every passive income stream that you create will go away forever. Nothing lasts forever. It is the law of life.

I am a great believer in the power of passive income. But one has to be a realist. Eventually the passive income flow you create will disappear one day. This is why it is important to create multiple sources of passive income. If you create large number of income streams they will be in different phases of growth, maturity and saturation stage. All your income streams will not dry out at once. Your cash flow will continue uninterrupted.

Even as you are enjoying benefits of one passive income stream you should be in search of new passive income streams. These are known as "growth activities." Once you create a passive income stream its maintenance will take very little of your time. You have to use your time creatively by engaging in growth activities to multiply your passive income streams.

8. Important Things to Remember

Before we jump into the conclusion, I just want to let you know that you are not restricted to choosing only one of the options from above. You are an entrepreneur - that means you are allowed to do whatever you want!

You can start an app development business and learn the ropes of building a successful app. After which, you can take that knowledge, write it into a book and publish it onto Amazon!

Nobody says that if you are a landlord, you have to look after your properties day in and day out, you can perhaps do some handicraft in your free time and put them on Etsy for sale! Be smart about what you can do, mix and match the different ways to achieve financial freedom.

Being a hustler means that you have to be street smart and resourceful. The greatest businessmen leverage on the things that they already have and turn them into greater things.

So now that you're at the end of this book, you've probably noticed a few things that we need to sum up. I'm going to give you the main points here, just so you walk away with them in mind and mull them over before you take any actions.

The first is that there is no truly passive income. You're going to have to work, especially at the beginning, for whatever it is you're looking to do. Whether you have to invest money into this or not is entirely up to what kind of route you're taking. But in the end, especially for those first few years, it's going to require time and elbow grease.

It is probably a good idea to save up at least 2 years worth of income before you quit your 9-5 job just so that it is enough to last you through the most difficult stages of building a successful passive income stream.

The second is that you need to have a plan about what you're doing and this can only formulate with research. Yes, it's very tantalizing to just jump in and get to work, and many people probably do that, but I beseech you not to go in all the way. Just wade in up to your hips and focus on having a plan. Call it experimenting if you have to, but don't go in guns blazing and eyes closed.

Be smart and knowledgeable about whatever it is you're doing. Know the market, know what you're going to provide, and know how to get it done. I have to admit that sometimes, it is impossible to know everything.

If you are building an app and have done all the possible validation there is to do, then there is no point trying to further prove that your product works. When something like this happens, do not doubt yourself. Sometimes all we need is a little bit of guts and just do it. After all, if we already know everything, what is the fun in life?

The third point is that you need to be passionate about whatever you're doing. Whether you're the next eBook sensation or you're going to open up a cheap mechanic shop for lawn mowers in your garage, you need to be passionate about it. Yes, we are all out here to make money. But we should never compromise our happiness in the process.

If you are an author and you hate writing books, imagine the long miserable hours you have to spend typing out pages of texts. Life is too short to feel miserable. In a nutshell, money should not be the deciding factor in your decision. If money is your primary goal, you're going to give up and burn out immediately. So get fired up about what you're doing!

The fourth point is that you're going to need to invest time in marketing and getting the word out that you're a business or that you have a product to sell. No one is going to know that you have a rental property waiting if you don't get a sign or that you have the best soap east of the Rockies if you don't tell them. So don't expect the customers to come to you, go find them and tell them what they're missing out on.

Finally, you have to know that this isn't an exhaustive list of what is possible. You can design homemade videogames; you can take paid surveys online, starting up an eBay company, sell a digital product or create thousand different things. The bottom line is that you have limitless opportunities that are only hidden from you by your lack of ambition and creativity. So get out there, keep learning and start working.

Start making money in your free time so that you can escape the 9-5 life. Build the life that you always wanted and enjoy the freedom that it brings.

Conclusion

I simply cannot over emphasize the importance of making a shift from linear income where you trade your hours for money towards creating a passive income where money and systems work for you day in and day out whether you are physically present or not. This is perhaps the most important secret of wealth creation. If you carry one message from this book is that creating passive income is the most important step towards gaining financial freedom.

There will be challenges along the way as you will need to shift your thinking and acquire new skills. You will radiate with joy and confidence when you see small streams of income joining into becoming full flow of residual cash flow that will bring prosperity to your family and loved ones for generations to come.

Good luck and get to work!